thoughts

and

observations

larry winget

thoughts and observations

By
Larry Winget
Copyright © MMII

thoughts and observations™ is a trademark of Win Publications!, Win Seminars!, and Larry Winget denoting a series of products that may include but is not limited to books, audio cassettes, video tapes, pocket cards, calendars, T-shirts, coffee mugs and more.

Published by:
Win Publications!
A subsidiary of Win Seminars!, Inc.
Tulsa, Oklahoma • Scottsdale, Arizona
www.larrywinget.com
800.749.4597

Printed in the United States of America.
Cover design and layout by Ad Graphics, Tulsa, Oklahoma.
Cover photo by Rose Mary Winget

ISBN: 1-881342-30-1

10 9 8 7 6 5 4 3 2 1

Here is something I think is interesting. There are actually people out there who won't buy this book because it has a picture of me on the cover smoking a cigar with a bottle of tequila on the table in front of me. They are going to judge the quality of what I have to say by the fact that I smoke cigars and enjoy a drink from time to time. In fact, when I told people about the cover picture before I printed the book they told me that some would be offended by it. Isn't that interesting? Actually I think it is just sad.

When I was in my early twenties I had a beard and was a telephone operator in Muskogee, Oklahoma while going to college. I wanted to transfer to the business office and was told that I would have to shave my beard. I asked them if they were more interested in how much hair I had on my face than they were in what came out of my face? They said yes. I shaved. I was easier then. And broker. I needed the job and the money. Now I just don't care.

Try this: If it isn't personally hurting you – then mind your own business. If you don't like someone then just don't be around them – don't do business with them – don't hire them. But don't feel compelled to judge them based only on how they look.

If someone is doing something you don't approve of and it has no effect on your life, then what do you care? Leave them alone. They are choosing to live that way. You get to choose to live your way.

But don't discount that person's value. Some of the best things ever invented or created were done so by really weird subversive people – take Christianity. Gotcha.

Empty. All used up. My epitaph. That's what will be on my tombstone. It means that if you can eat it, I've eaten it. If you can drive it, I've driven it. If you can ride it, I've ridden it. If you can read it, I've read it. If you can listen to it, I've heard it. If you can say it, I've said it. If it can be done, I've done it. I don't want to die with things still left to do. And though that will happen, I want to spend the time I have doing everything I ever dreamed of doing.

You can tell a lot about a person by the music they listen to. Ask someone their favorite artist. (Mine's Elvis.) Their favorite song. (Mine is "Unchained Melody.") Their top five artists. (Mine are Elvis, Van Morrison, Leon Russell, Merle Haggard, and Willie Nelson.) You can pretty much tell when they grew up, where they grew up, what kind of person they are and more all by the music they like best. I think that's interesting. By the way, a list of only five was too short for me. So I am going to add George Jones and Tom Jones (not brothers, by the way) into my top five list.

larry winget

Smoking. If you choose to die that way I don't care. It is your God-given right and privilege. Just be courteous about it. And another thing, don't throw your cigarette butt on the ground. Unless you are really hardcore and smoke filterless cigarettes, then your butt will be there for a good long while before it breaks down or until someone picks it up.

Yes, I smoke cigars. I know the health risks. And I do it mostly in the privacy of my own home so as not to offend. Thanks for your concern.

My Philosophy of Life

Expect the best.
Be prepared for the worst.
Celebrate it all.

larry winget

Life is short. Way too short and getting shorter every day it seems. So enjoy it. Become an absolute hedonist and just enjoy it. Stop being so self-righteous and pious and get your panties out of a wad and just kick back and enjoy it. No one really cares that much any way. I promise. And if they do...........screw 'em. What do you care what people think??? And who are they to judge you? So get on with your life and enjoy it – there's not much time left.

At the end of the day what really matters? A guy asked me that yesterday during an interview. It was the best question I have ever been asked in an interview. Know what I answered? Of course you don't, so let me tell you: Not much. Really, not much matters. At the end of the day if you smiled more than you frowned, laughed more than cried, told your family and friends that you loved them and had a pretty good time doing what you do for a living, then it was a good day. Go to bed and say thanks. That's about it.

Friends. You don't need too many. That's never been a real problem for me. I've never had very many. It's not easy being my friend. I am what you call "hard to get along with." So when someone is my friend, it's because they want to be. And I appreciate that. I love my friends. I will do what it takes to help them. Period. No judgment. No BS. No questions asked. I think that is what a friend is.

I don't ask much. If you make me a promise, keep it. If you give me your word, don't go back on it. If you say you are going to be there, be there - and be there when you said you would. If you mess up, admit it and accept the consequences. And if I am giving you money for a product or service, be at least a little grateful and smile at me some. That's all I ask.

larry winget

Money. People say that money is over rated. No it isn't. Having money is a lot better than not having money. I like having it. I can do a lot of stuff with it that I could never do without it. So don't put money down. Don't joke about being broke. It isn't funny. Don't make fun of people who have it. As Reverend Ike says, "Make fun of the rich and you won't be one of us." Money is a good thing. You can't build hospitals, schools, churches, help the homeless, feed the hungry, or be charitable in any way without money. Earn as much of it as you can, give away as much of it as you can and spend as much of it as you can.

My last meal. Ever think about that? I do all the time. Not that I am on death row or anything but I still think about it a lot. So what would yours be? Mine would be chicken fried steak, mashed potatoes and gravy, fried okra, two fried eggs, fried apples, chocolate pie, iced tea and coffee. Can you tell where I am from?? And I know that it's all fried. Hey, it's my last meal so what do I care about cholesterol?

Kids. Most of their lives they are pretty much a pain in the butt. There. It's been said. They are dirty, messy and expensive. They keep you from doing what you would like to do so you can drive them to do what they want to do. And yet they are still about the coolest things on the planet. I love mine. I may not like yours, but I love mine. And you may not like mine, but I bet you love yours too. And do you know the most important thing I have learned about kids? They grow out of it. Write that down. That's my best piece of parenting advice. They grow out of it.

Want to make me really mad? Honk at me. That's all it takes. I hate to be honked at. When I am in the left hand turn lane and the light begins to change, just because I am not halfway through the intersection before the red fades and the green begins to glow does not mean that I am not paying attention. So don't honk at me. A guy did that not long ago and I put my car in park and got out and walked back to his car and politely asked what it was he wanted. I do things like that. People think I'm crazy. Then they leave me alone. I like that. But I don't like it when people honk at me.

Have you ever heard people say, "If I had a nickel for everytime I...."? The truth is if they really had a nickel for everytime that thing happened, they would have about thirty-five cents.

Affection that comes from lack of obligation is the sweetest and most meaningful.

I think that there should be a mandatory driver's test for anyone over seventy years old. I will happily submit to one when I get there. Check the statistics – or just take a drive in Miami, Palm Springs or Scottsdale during the winter when the snowbirds are in town. If you do, then you will agree with me.

Be quiet at the movies. Don't talk once the lights go down. I mean at all! You are not in your living room and you are not watching a video. You are surrounded by people who paid way too much to be there and we don't want to hear you or your comments. Don't chew too loud. Don't let your candy wrapper make noise. Don't dig around in the bottom of the popcorn box like a gerbil. And if someone politely asks you to be quiet, then be quiet. Otherwise I will call the manager and have your sorry butt thrown out. And please get there on time. You know what time the show started. It was in the paper. You looked it up so you could go to the movie in the first place. So get there on time so you don't have to stumble over me in the dark. And please don't leave your pager or cell phone on. Please.

Better to have a good divorce than a bad marriage.

When I was forty I got my ear pierced. A little old to do that you might say. Yeah well, when you are forty I figure you are old enough to do what you damn well please. A lot of people don't like it. Tough. Some people won't even hire me because of it. I don't care.

Gaseous emittances (farting.) Don't think that yours don't stink – they do. So don't think that we can't smell it. We can. And we know that you are the one who did it. And you might just be around someone like me when you do it, which means that someone will say something rude to you about your doing it and it will be said very loudly for all to hear in order to embarrass you.

My wife and I were at the movies when a huge woman in the aisle behind us decided that she needed to go to the restroom. You can exit an aisle either by facing the screen, the more common practice, or by facing the people who are seated. She decided to use the latter way to exit meaning that her big butt hit the head of every single person in the row in front of her (my row.) When she got to where I was, she paused to step around some packages on the floor and with her butt right between my wife and me and when she did, let a big one. The woman next to me said, "I wonder if she thought we wouldn't notice?"

By the way, there is nothing in the world funnier than a fart. It's a guy thing.

From a bus driver in Dublin, Ireland:

A guy discovers that his grandfather has died and immediately calls his grandmother to offer his condolences. His grandmother proceeds to tell him that he died while they were having sex. The man is amazed and exclaims, "But Grandma, you are 90 and he was 93!" She said, "I know, we were only able to do it once a week. We did it on Sunday mornings. He kept his rhythm by listening to the church bells down the street, you know, Dong - - - Dong - - - Dong - - - Dong, in fact, he would be alive today if it weren't for the ice cream truck."

Tattoos. They are addictive. If you get one you will want more. I have five. I want more. I'm old enough to decide so don't give me your viewpoints or opinions. I don't live with you and you don't have to see me. My wife does, her opinion counts, not yours. The only suggestion I have about tattoos is to only get them in places that you can cover when dressed in long sleeves and long pants. And only get something that you are not going to be ashamed to show your mother.

Family. Who says that you have to get along with them? You didn't pick them. You were born with them. Now luckily I get along with all of mine – but that's just luck. Just because you are related to someone does not mean that you are going to be like them or enjoy their company. What about the old line, "Blood is thicker that water?" You are right. It is. But so is gravy.

Romance your partner or someone else will.

Men are pigs. Men, don't argue with it. It's true. Stop kidding yourself. Stop trying to deny it. Instead accept it, learn to control it and live with it without being totally repulsive to the rest of the world.

Women. Live with it. It is what we are. Love us in spite of it. Forgive us for it.

If it were up to men, all women would wear leather miniskirts, thigh high stockings, spike heels and halter-tops.

If it were up to men, beer would come from a tap in the kitchen like water. Men think the best piece of furniture ever invented is the Lazy-boy recliner. In leather. Men are positive about the fact that the television remote control is the best invention of all time.

Men like lingerie. And who ever Victoria is, we love her Secret. She should be given an Oscar, an Emmy, a Tony, the Medal Of Freedom, a Purple Heart, the Nobel Peace Prize, a Pulitzer, the Congressional Medal Of Honor, and all the gold in Fort Knox. On the other hand, Laura Ashley is the Antichrist. See? We are pigs!

Men like cartoons.

On the other hand. Men like to be asked how we feel and what we think. We like to be complimented on how we look and what we have on. We are sensitive. We cry. We hurt. We like clothes. Not all of us like sports. We may be pigs but a few of us are actually people – and most of us are pretty good guys.

 True happiness comes when you rise above the approval and acceptance of others and instead approve of and accept yourself.

I think everyone should be happy. I'm happy. I hope you are too. But don't rub my nose in your happiness, okay? Most of us are out there leading normal lives and the last thing we want is Little Miss (or Mister) Sunshine in our face telling us to have a superfantastic day. You know exactly the people I am talking about. Like those people who work for Disney. "Have a magical day!" I want to choke them. I stayed at one of the Disney hotels in Orlando a week or so ago and in the first thirty minutes after checking in I received four calls to my room from various hotel people welcoming me and wanting to find out if my check-in went okay and then to find out if my room was satisfactory and then from the manager a voice mail offering to do whatever it takes to make my stay a magical one. Here's an idea, if you want to make my stay more magical, quit calling me and put something other than Disney movies on Spectravision and put some scotch in my mini-bar. It's called a mini-BAR for a reason. Some would say that what they were doing is just good service. No, that isn't good service. It is annoying. Some people confuse good service with pestering people. You've experienced the overly helpful clerk; the one who hovers over you saying how good that would look on you and can I find your size and on and on and on. Wait. I could get really carried away on this one so I'll stop now. And have a magical day.

Avoid doctors who are fat, who smoke, who recommend drugs to lose weight, and who make you wait more than 30 minutes to see them.

Okay, if a place only has two sizes of drink – then they CAN'T be medium and large. One of them HAS to be a small. But try to order a small when they only have two sizes: medium and large. You can't do it. They will argue with you. "We only have medium and large." No. With only two sizes, ONE is small. You can ONLY have a medium when there are three sizes, not two. Medium means the one in the middle. And take that same logic to Starbuck's. Their small is a tall. Figure that one out.

Don't go to a church where the minister tells you that you are anything less than perfect. You are not a miserable worthless sinner. That is crap and it is not what God would say.

larry winget

If a hotel is described as quaint that means it won't have Spectra Vision or a mini-bar. Room service, if they have it, will close at some ridiculously early hour. The furniture will be old. There won't be a place to plug your computer in unless you move the bed away from the wall. And many times, there won't even be a shower. How quaint. I'll take Caesar's Palace any time.

Did you ever notice that places that serve anything made of dough or caffeine (like bagel and coffee places) are full of stupid people? Those ingredients seem to affect people's brains. I am a smart guy and do pretty well in life but I have no idea where to stand in line, where to pay, or where to wait for my coffee. There are no signs and the people who work there are as clueless as I seem to be.

Don't be noisy. Don't whistle, hum, sing to yourself, talk to yourself, talk to everyone around you, make obnoxious tapping, clicking, snapping noises, or pop your chewing gum. This goes double for when you are in closed areas like elevators, when standing in line behind someone, or when on an airplane.

Do not talk to someone else while you have me on the phone. That is rude. Do not take another call while you have me on the phone unless I give you my permission, which I won't. Do not eat while you are having a conversation on the telephone.

When I go out to dinner with a group of people, I think the right and easy thing to do when the check comes is to just divide it by the number of people there and to pay up. I hate it when someone says, "but I only had........." That bugs the crap out of me. Just be a big boy or girl and pay your part. In the long run it all evens out and you won't look like a cheapskate.

As a guy who spends almost every day of his life in an airport and on an airplane, let me assure you: your airports and airplanes are not safer. Sorry. All that the added security has done is piss people off. It hasn't made anyone safer. In fact, I think it is more dangerous to fly now than ever before. Now you have an airplane full of irate passengers who have just been subjected to having their underwear dragged out on a table for everyone to see just to find a pair of tweezers. I have seen them stand ninety-year-old ladies up out of their wheelchairs to frisk them. I have seen them tear apart a Barbie bag belonging to a six-year-old little girl looking for something dangerous. I have been searched so many times I have lost track. I have been told that it was an FAA regulation to turn on my computer. It is NOT an FAA regulation to turn it on. I have been told that my carry-on could not be carried on because it weighed more than twenty-two pounds and that was a strictly enforced FAA regulation as well. It is not an FAA regulation and no one has ever heard of it except for the one ticket agent at Air Canada that weighed only MY carry-on. If carry-on bags over twenty-two pounds were not allowed you would have to pull about ninety percent of the carry-on bags off of every plane. Wait, I just figured it out. She was probably using the Canadian/American exchange rate: twenty-two pounds American would be about forty pounds Canadian and that's heavy! I have also been told that my cigar cutter was a weapon and that I couldn't take it on the plane even though I carried it on at least one hundred times since September 11 with no problem. I asked how it could be a weapon unless I decided to clip the end off of the pilot's nose, or got him to stick his finger in it or convinced him to hold still for an amateur bris. (This one got ugly – it was a forty-dollar cigar cutter – and they ended up keeping it.) I was even asked about the plungers I carry as speech props. When I told them that I made a living sticking them on my head, they told me they did not tolerate jokes. I told them that must make it hard to come to work every day then. They didn't get it. When you read about airplane rage, it is probably the airline that has caused it. Because it is an outRAGEously stupid process that is only getting worse. People should be searched, but let's use some common sense, consistency and brains. And let's make THAT an FAA regulation.

Las Vegas. I love it. It is loud, noisy, tacky, obnoxious, stays up all night, is stuffed with excellent food and is a little bit naughty. Vegas.......it's ME!

I have decided to change my name to Random. Because at the airport, when they announce that there is going to be a random search it always means me.

When someone works for you pay them a good wage. Don't expect someone else to help you get rich while you keep them broke. And never mess with someone's money. Ever.

Never lie. My Dad always said he would rather have a thief than a liar working for him because at least you could watch a thief. Sometimes telling the truth is hard. And the consequences are hard. But they are never as hard as living with a lie.

Read. People just don't read. I have talked about this in nearly all my books. But no one read them so who remembers? What's really interesting is that book sales are up. New book stores are being built nearly every day. Know why? Good coffee. No one is reading the books – they buy them and they drink the coffee but few people actually take the time to read the books. I just read that people on the average read about 100 hours a year and watch television about 2000 hours a year. Almost 40 hours a week watching TV and less than 2 hours a week reading anything. Is it any wonder that people are so stupid?

Stupidity. I have no tolerance for it. There is no excuse. Education is free. Stupidity is a choice. You aren't stupid by accident. You have chosen not to pay attention and learn something. No slack for you.

The Truth hurts. That is how you know it's the truth. If someone says something really sweet to you, they are probably lying.

When I was a little boy growing up across from the Round-up Club in Muskogee, Oklahoma, and watching The Lone Ranger and Roy Rogers and John Wayne, I fell in love with cowboy boots. I wore them a lot as a little kid while pretending to be riding the plains. There has never been a time in my life when I didn't have a pair of cowboy boots. However, I rarely wore them. Somehow when you wear cowboy boots people think you are a cowboy. I'm not. That really isn't fair though. I wear tennis shoes and I don't play tennis. I wear running shoes and I don't run. I have even worn Bass Weejuns and I'm not a Bass or a Weejun. (What is a Weejun anyway?) But because I didn't want to be thought of as a cowboy I just didn't wear my boots much. But I don't care what anyone thinks any more so I wear cowboy boots almost exclusively now. Wearing them somehow almost makes me feel like a little boy again watching The Lone Ranger. I now have around thirty pairs of boots. (I am prone to be a bit excessive. I used to have sixty-five pairs of eyeglasses.) And now when I wonder whether my boots are in style, I remember a quote by Raquel Welch: "Style is being yourself on purpose." Consequently I know, my boots are in style. "Hi-yo Silver.... away!"

Perception is reality. That is so wrong yet I hear people say it all the time. Perception is NOT reality. Reality is reality. People used to believe that the world was flat. That was their perception. It was not reality. It was just their reality. Reality was that the world was round. Be careful when you hear that perception is reality because it might just be perception.

Cynicism. I get accused of being a cynic. Good. We need cynicism. If people would have had a little more cynicism then we would not have had the Branch Davidians, or the mass suicides surrounding Jim Jones, or all of the people being duped by Jim Bakker and his kind or the issues that the Catholics are facing with their priests right now. We MUST question everything. Religion, authority, politicians, the government, laws........everything. And yes, I did mean to include religion. God can handle the cynicism and the questioning; religion has the problem with it.

Toupees. Just don't. We can always tell. We can tell with the plugs and implants and all of the other fake hair stuff too. So, I mean it, please, just don't.

The Beatles were right.

Love is all there is.

I love my dog. In fact, I love everyone's dog. I like people's dogs much more than I like them. (If you are a dog person, you will understand that statement.) Dogs always love you. They never judge you. You can do about anything and your dog will still worship you. Will your spouse or kids or friends or coworkers do that? Nope. Only your dog. Your cat won't. They hold grudges and get even. But not your dog. I love my dog. My current dog is named Butter. Butter the French Bulldog. Not the smartest dog in the world. A strong C student though. I've had Elvis, an English Bulldog. A struggling D student. Nixon a German Shepherd, a brilliant A student. And yet, intelligence never really mattered much. Smart or stupid they only wanted to be petted and played with. And no matter how smart or stupid they were they still drank out of the toilet.

The less people have to say, the more they feel compelled to say it.

Discover your uniqueness and learn to exploit it in the service of others and you are guaranteed success, happiness and prosperity.

Without exception that is the smartest thing I ever said.

As I sit writing this I am in my hotel room in Maui in Hawaii. I am in Hawaii a lot. Nice place. The whale watching is a cool thing to do and anyplace that has women in bikinis is fine by me. It just takes too long to get here. Which makes me wonder how it ended up as a state. Why did the United States have to travel this far to get another state? Why didn't we pick some place closer? Like Toronto? Don't get me wrong, it's a great place and I appreciate the Hawaiians and welcome their tax dollars and their votes and all that – but somehow if you've got to spend that many hours on a plane getting some-place, when you get there it ought to be a foreign country. You would appreciate the flight more I think if you ended up in a foreign country.

thoughts and observations

I have discovered that very few places in this country know what barbeque is. First, it is not what you do on your grill in the backyard. It always bothers me when someone says that they are going to have a barbeque. You don't *have* a barbeque, you *eat* barbeque. In most instances it is a noun, not a verb. You are cooking out, or grilling, but you are not barbequeing (the verb) unless you are basting the meat over a bed of charcoal or some other type of fire in some sauce that is made up of brown sugar, tomatoes (ketchup), a little vinegar and some spices. Second, in my opinion only Texans and Oklahomans know what barbeque really is. The people in Kansas City think that they have the market cornered on barbeque but I think they have missed the boat. Kansas barbeque has a sauce that is vinegar based and is very tangy. In Oklahoma and Texas, they have a tomato based sauce that is sweeter. I like it sweet. But at least the people in Kansas City have sauce. When you go to the Carolinas or that general area of the South, the barbeque is dry. What is that about? You don't even get messy eating it. So in my opinion, which has *never* been humble by any stretch of the imagination, if you want good barbeque, head for Oklahoma or Texas.

I am tired of helping people who need help. I have done it for years. One example of that is the help I have given beginning speakers who desperately needed to know how to become successful in the speaking business. No more. People who need help rarely appreciate the help or do anything with it. So I am going to quit helping those who need it. Instead I am going to only help people who want help. There is a big difference. People who want help appreciate it when you help them and usually will actually use the help. So if you need anything from me, don't bother calling. If you want something, then we'll talk.

My boys and I have always played a game based on the idea "what would you do for how much money." Stupid stuff like how much money would it take for you to eat a worm or to bite the head off of a rat and things like that. (My price is always much cheaper than theirs by the way; I know what it takes to make the big bucks and somehow a worm and a rat head don't seem like that big of a deal to me.) When my boys were about 5 and 9, we were taking our dogs, Elvis and Nixon for a walk. I had some dog biscuits in my pocket and I asked my son Tyler what he would take to eat a dog biscuit. He said he would eat one if I did. So I popped it in my mouth, chewed it up and swallowed it with a smile and then handed him his. He wouldn't do it. I explained to him the principle of "A deal is a deal." I wouldn't let him off the hook. We stood right there in the middle of the street for a good long while with him saying no because he didn't really mean it. I then explained the meaning of the saying, "don't let your mouth write a check that your butt can't cash." I told him that we would stand there all night if we had to but that he was going to eat that dog biscuit. Finally, reluctantly, he did. Some would say that I am a harsh father. I think that was one of the best learning experiences of his life. As a man now, we look back at that event and laugh about it and he agrees. Most people never learn the lesson of "a deal is a deal" and daily write checks that their butt can't cash. I think they should have to eat a dog biscuit.

Are you afraid of dying? I am. I am not afraid of being dead. But that's a whole lot different than being afraid of dying. I just don't want to go through the experience of actually dying. Because regardless of how much you want to quietly go in your sleep, that rarely happens. Besides, that wouldn't really be my style anyway. That's what scares me. I don't like blood and guts especially when they are mine. And I don't like hospitals or being sick or disease or pain. See why I am afraid? I wish you could just skip the dying part and go straight to being dead.

Guymon, Oklahoma. Every state has one. You know the kind of place that when it's about seventy-five degrees everywhere else in the state, it is fifteen there? In Kansas, it's Goodland. In Arizona, it's Flagstaff. Flagstaff has mountains so they have an excuse. But it's always the same it seems, I watch the meteorologist come on and report that Phoenix is ninety-eight degrees and sure enough Flagstaff will be about twenty. Actually it is pretty stupid to even have a meteorologist in Arizona. They could actually just come out and say, "Okay, you remember today? Well, it's pretty much going to be exactly like that tomorrow." The weather doesn't change much. Except for Monsoon Season. When I heard about the dreaded Monsoon Season I had no idea what to expect. Then I lived through my first one. They should rename it the Cloudy Season. When your annual rainfall is seven inches it is ridiculous to use the word monsoon at all. Unless you live in Guymon.

Computers drive me crazy. I am a Mac guy. Supposedly the easiest computer on earth to use. And it is. I like my Mac. And it still drives me crazy. Does your computer drive you crazy? I think mine has a personality. And it hates me. And it beats me up about every other week. It decides to just stop doing all the stuff that it did just the day before. Why does it do that? And where is the stuff that I just saved? Where? And why is it that when I put a new program on, the old ones don't like it? Even right now, as I write this book and am trying to print it out, the computer is telling me that it can't find the printer. Why not? It's setting right there not five feet away. It's in the same spot it was ten minutes ago when

you used it to print so why can't you find it now?
Did you forget?

About once a year mine gets so screwed up that
I just put it in a box and buy a new one. Really
I do. I used to call the tech help line. And after
about a 3 hour wait on hold they got so frus-
trated with me that they would put me on hold
to scream and conveniently cut me off, knowing that I wouldn't call back. I even tried a few
times to hire a guy to come over to my house to
fix my problems. They talked in a language that
I just couldn't understand. So what does this
mean? Nothing. But buy Apple stock. I am a
great customer.

I can honestly say that I have no prejudice against, race, color, religious affiliation or lack of, sexual orientation, or anything else that you can think of that you have no control over. Now regarding those things that you do have control over – that's another story. These are my big prejudices: stupid, lazy and rude. That's because you can fix any one of those. You are stupid, lazy or rude by choice. And God help you if you are all of those things. And I meant what I just said: God help you. Because I won't.

So if you have a tendency to be a prejudiced person, and you know if you are, then I suggest that you change your prejudices from things that people can't control to things that people can control. Like your own prejudice. Maybe I could control mine against stupid, lazy and rude. Naah.

Funerals. Funerals seem to be more for the living, and not the dead. I am going to be cremated and have my ashes put in an Elvis Jim Beam bottle. I already have the bottle. My family has even reluctantly agreed to it. But no one wants the bottle. You want it? You can have me. On your mantle. Just call my wife and arrange it.

Kids should be seen and not heard. You've heard that before. Actually a better statement is: Neighbors should be seen and not heard. That makes much more sense to me.

Did you ever notice that when someone says, "I only have one thing to say........" it isn't true? They always have much more than only one thing to say.

Don't ever say anything stupid like, "It can't get any worse than this." That is a challenge you do not want to issue to the Universe. Trust me, if there is one thing it can always get, It can get worse!

If you are unhappy, unsuccessful, sick or broke, please just keep it to yourself; the rest of us don't want or need to hear it. Don't feel compelled to share.

I walked into a meeting room where I was about to speak and the meeting planner said to me, "Are you going to make sure that we have a good time?" I told her no, I was going to make sure that I have a good time. Because if I am having a good time then others will most likely want to join me, but if I'm not having any fun, nobody is going to have any fun. I learned a long time ago that you cannot be responsible for anyone enjoying life except for yourself. It's not up to you to make anyone else happy. It's only up to you to make you happy. Will this work for everyone? It works for me.

Results are everything and they never lie.

Sex is the coolest thing on the planet and our society has done its best to make it wrong and dirty. We try to legislate it. That doesn't work. We try to limit it. That doesn't work. We try to make it appear nasty so people won't want to do it so much. That doesn't work. In fact, that only makes people want to do it more. So what is the answer? More sex. There isn't one thing in this world wrong with it so just go ahead and give yourself permission to do it and to enjoy it. In fact: Do it whenever you can, wherever you can, and as much as you can until the day you die. And remember this about sex: If you ain't sweatin', you are doing something wrong. Now if this little observation offends you, it's probably because you aren't getting any.

Stress comes from knowing what is right and doing what is wrong. Everyone already knows the right thing to do. The problem is that we don't do it. We do the wrong thing. That is what causes the stress. Doing the wrong thing when we know what the right thing is. People go to stress management seminars. What a waste of time. Why would you want to learn to manage something you don't even want? So if you want to live a stress free life, just do what you know is right.

Women are like houses. They aren't really interesting until they get a few years on them. It is the wear and tear that gives them character and makes them more interesting. And the older ones, when fixed up with love and care are always the most beautiful, the most sought after and the most expensive. While the new ones are fun to look at and even fun to tour from time to time, and maybe even rent for a while, you really wouldn't want to live there.

Few people will turn to themselves to take responsibility for their results until they have exhausted all opportunities to blame someone else.

Learn to be selfish. I know that you have been told your whole life NOT to be selfish. But they were wrong. You should share your money and your stuff but learn to be selfish with yourself. Your first obligation is to yourself. You can't be any good for someone else unless you are first good to yourself. Take care of yourself. Then go share who you are with the world.

The most broken commandment of the Big Ten: Thou shalt not steal. You may say that you are not a thief but I bet you are. Any time you give less than your best, then you have stolen from your employer, your customers, your coworkers, the world and mostly from yourself. You must always give your very best. Good enough, isn't.

Style. Have some. If you don't have any – buy some. But somewhere, somehow, get some. Never go anyplace where they won't remember you were there. Make a statement.

Don't be different. People are afraid of different. People won't pay for different. Instead be unique. People pay a premium for unique.

The stranger you are, the better you have to be. That's why I have to be really good.

larry winget

You know what bugs me? Other than almost everything? A lousy handshake. One of those dead fish things that some people give you. Especially women. Women, who taught you that? Do you think that's feminine? It isn't. It's..............just yuk. Grab the other person's hand and give it a good shake. Don't pump it, you will appear rural. And don't try to crush the other person's knuckles. Just make sure that the web between your thumb and forefinger touches the web between their thumb and forefinger and give one or two shakes with a firm grip. That's it. Not that hard to do yet it makes such a good first impression.

The sexiest thing on a woman
(or a man) is confidence.

larry winget

Three men are sitting naked in the sauna. Suddenly there is a beeping sound. The first man presses his forearm and the beeping stops. The others look at him curiously. "That's my pager," he says. "I have a microchip under the skin of my arm." A few minutes later a phone rings. The second man lifts his palm to his ear. When he finishes he explains, "That's my cellular phone. I have a microchip in my hand." The third man, feeling decidedly low-tech, steps out of the sauna. In a few minutes he returns with a piece of toilet paper extending from his rear. The others raise their eyebrows. "I'm getting a Fax," he explains.

At this time of this writing, I am almost 50 years old. I don't feel that old. I heard someone ask the question the other day, "How old would you be if you didn't know how old you were?" I like that question. How old would you be? I'd be 25. That's how old my attitude is and that's how old I feel inside. Thank God I'm not that stupid though. I've learned some things since then – not that I always do the smart thing – but at least I know better now. I saw an interview with Cher the other day and the interviewer asked her what was good about growing older. I loved her answer. She said, "Not a damn thing." I am tired of people who talk about how great getting old is. What's so great about it? My back hurts, I wake up groaning, my feet get tired and my hangovers last a lot longer than they used to. I'm smarter but it seems like there should be a better way to get smart without having to get old. I hope someone figures it out.

larry winget

When in doubt, wear black.

I watched again the other day the movie "Ali" with Will Smith. I have always been a big fan of Ali and boxing and thought they did a good job. And I think that Jamie Foxx did an outstanding job as Bundini Brown. But in the movie when Ali was just so amazed at the response he was receiving after making some of his somewhat controversial statements, he said, "Man this is just unreal." To which I think it was Bundini who said, "The more real you get the more unreal it's gonna get." And that's my point. Very few people are ever willing to be real. Yet that is when life gets interesting. In my life and career, when I quit giving the speech the meeting planner wanted and the company who hired me said they wanted and just started being myself and giving the speech I wanted to give, my career went crazy. . . became unreal. All because I was willing to be real. I suggest this that this is a good idea for everyone and every business. Who are you? If you know, then just be that. Unless you are a jerk. If you are a jerk, be someone else.

I have two boys. You have probably heard me talk about them in my speeches. Tyler, the older of the two, is a sniper/paratrooper in the 82nd Airborne in the United States Army stationed in Fort Bragg, North Carolina. Patrick is a fashion design major at the Fashion Institute of Design and Merchandising in Los Angeles, California. One is a trained killer and one is a fashion designer. Both pretty much the purest forms of my personality. My neck is red but my heart is lavender. Tyler does what he does because he likes to fight. Patrick does what he does because he likes tall, skinny women. So different yet they both came from me. How does that happen?

Funny thing about success: People want you to be successful – just not more successful than they are.

The Big Questions Of Life

Am I happy?
Am I healthy?
Am I serving?
Am I loving?
Am I learning?
Am I having fun?
Am I doing something I enjoy?
Am I prosperous?

If the answer to all of these questions
is yes, then celebrate.

If the answer to any of these questions
is no, then do something immediately
to change things in your life.

When you go in a clothing store and see fifteen of the same item and know that there are two hundred other stores in that chain and there are at least three other chains with that many more stores carrying the same item with at least that much inventory of that item, consider that a clue NOT to buy that item. It doesn't say that it is in style as much as it says that it will soon be out of style.

I went to see Tom Jones in Vegas a while back. The man is in his mid-sixties and has three generations of women throwing their panties at him. I have never had even one generation of women do that. Hell, I've never even had one woman do that. I don't think that's fair. But he sounds better than ever and still looks pretty good too. Hope they still say that about me in fifteen years.

If your life sucks, it is because you suck.

Go out and buy every book you can find by Nelson DeMille and read them (every book except for *Spencerville* and *Plum Island*). And then buy some Stephen King. For the high brows who think he only writes horror, you are missing one of the best story tellers of our time or any other time. He scares me and makes me laugh and cry. And if you are in any kind of creative position professionally, then read *Stephen King on Writing*. It teaches you how to tell a story and grab people's emotions. And don't go to bed tonight without buying and starting my favorite fiction book of all time, *A Prayer For Owen Meany* by John Irving. Remember that life is short and you must read as many books as you can. Don't have time? Turn off the television.

The best thing ever put on film has to be *Lonesome Dove*. The book by Larry McMurtry was great but this is one time that the movie more than did the book justice. A story of friendship like none other. My favorite line is when Gus is lying on his death bed and he turns to Woodrow, his best friend for so many years and says, "By God, Woodrow, it's been a party ain't it?" I cry every time. And that's what I want my last words to my sweet wife Rose Mary to be, "It's been a party ain't it?"

Give up hope. Hope has never done you a bit of good. To me, hope says that you wish something would happen the way you want it to, but it could just as easily not. Kind of like shooting craps only the odds aren't as good. You don't need hope. You need faith. Faith says that you BELIEVE something will happen and you have no doubt about it. Hope is mixed with uncertainty. Faith is grounded in absolute certainty. Now which is most powerful? When you have hope, you also have doubt. When you have faith, there is no doubt. And who is willing to take action on something that could just as easily not come about as come about? Not me. And I don't think you would either. I believe it is much easier to take action on what you KNOW is true! It is easier to get up off your butt and do something when you are sure of the outcome. And when you have faith – that unshakable belief that what you know, you KNOW that you know, then it isn't hard at all to do what it takes to see your faith turn into something tangible. Give up hope and cling to belief and faith.

We all spend most of our lives trying to figure out how to get more. You get more by giving up more. That is the irony. You only get by giving up. You lose weight by giving up the stuff that isn't good for you to eat. You get rich by giving up the stuff that keeps you from getting rich. Things like too much television, lousy work habits, not reading, etc. You get more successful by giving up the stuff that keeps you from being successful. That is how it works. Give up the stuff that is stopping you from getting what you want and you will get what you want.

W hat have you taught your children? I have taught mine what a good hamburger is and what great barbeque is. They both got that. Other than those two important things, they picked and chose the other things they wanted to learn from me. Tyler takes responsibility. When he messes up, he admits it. Patrick has discovered his uniqueness. He isn't afraid to be different and is completely confident in his individuality. I admire my boys. I have taught them important things. Just as they have taught me important things. Thanks guys, I love you both.

When you mess up, big deal. Just admit it, fix it and move one. Other than that, life is a party.

That's the smartest thing my son, Tyler Winget, ever said.

larry winget

I never met anybody who didn't already know everything that it takes to be successful. We all already know. The problem is not that we don't know what to do. The problem is that we don't do what we know to do. The problem is not in the knowing – it is in the doing.

What I Believe.

Life is simple.

You can have anything you want.

You create your life: the good and the bad.

Love, service and giving must be the
motives of your life.

Money is easy and comes to you as the
result of serving others.

Service often comes disguised as work.

You can be healthy and don't have
to suffer sickness.

You live the life you choose to live.

You can change.

Words are powerful and shape the
circumstances of your life.

Thoughts are creative and control
your outcome.

Trust your feelings.

Whining and refusing to take responsibility kill your chances of success.

Results never lie.

Most people are lazy and need to get off
their butts and do something.

All good is rewarded.

Passion is a necessity for a happy life.

Guilt serves no purpose.

Worry is a waste of time and energy.

Personal satisfaction comes only when
you rise above the approval of others.

Everything in life gets better when you
get better and nothing gets better
until you get better.

When it comes to kids, remember: they grow out of it.

God is the Presence of Good and the Action of Love.

Love your work and by loving it you will become excellent at it and rewarded well for it.

It's wonderful to have lots of stuff, but it takes more than stuff to make you happy.

Fun should be a way of life, not something you have from time to time.

Everything in life is a lesson. Refusing to learn the lesson means that it will be repeated until the lesson is learned.

In the long run, none of this really matters much anyway so don't get your panties in a wad.

Guilt is a total waste of time. So forget guilt. It serves no purpose. You can't change what has already been done. You certainly can't change what is done by feeling bad about it. Forgive yourself, learn from the experience and decide to act differently next time.

Concerning guilty pleasures:

Never feel guilty about anything that gives you pleasure.

We spend our lives going to work and making money in order to figure out how we can live. That's backwards. Instead, figure out how you would like to live and then figure out how to work in order to make that happen. Choose your lifestyle first. Don't let your lifestyle be the result of what's left over every month.

What do a fundamentalist and a lobotomy have in common?

They are both no-brainers.

We board airplanes all wrong. We let first class board and then kids and then we start at the back of the plane. No good. We should board first class last. It isn't first class to be on the plane and have people stepping over you and it is stupid for them to try to serve drinks to the first class people when everyone else is boarding. That just slows things down even more. So, board the last rows first – only put the window seats on, then the middle seats and then the aisle seats. And people with kids do NOT get to board early. That is a dumb idea. It does not speed things up. The only people who can get on early are the people in wheel chairs or who have other physical infirmities. Okay, so now the plane is loaded from the back to the front and from the windows, to the middle seats to the aisle seats. Now, it is time to board first class. Dear Airlines: this will work. Try it. You don't even have to give me credit.

Time management. Another dumb idea made up by people trying to sell seminars. Who cares about managing time? Instead we should learn to manage our priorities. When you know what is the most important thing to do and then do it, time takes care of itself. The problem is we have not clearly defined our priorities. We don't know what is the most important thing to do. In my opinion, taking care of customers is the most important thing in business. When you do that, everything else falls into place. In your personal life, it is being happy and enjoying who you are and what you do. When you do that, the rest of it falls into place as well. See how simple life really is?

What is the last thing a redneck says before he dies?

"Hey, y'all watch this!"

larry winget

If you were in a Mexican jail, who would get you out? That is not a dumb question. Things happen. At least to me they do. Have you thought about it? I have. I know exactly who will be called. I have a friend, Mike Boyd who would spend whatever it takes to get me out of jail. My friend Larry Mudd, would show up and saw through the bars, if only his truck makes it there. My son, Tyler would be there with guns blazing along with two of his Army buddies, Floyd and Scruggs, to bust me out. My friend and manager of my business, Vic Osteen, would organize the whole event, rounding up all the resources and coordinating the efforts of every one to assure that the break out would come off as planned. My A.S.S. (American Speakers Society) buddies would show up, get the jailers drunk, tell them jokes and baffle them with BS, while some-one else actually did the work.

Who would get you out? My advice: Be prepared.

thoughts and observations

As you grow older you think more about God.
I'm not sure why that is but it seems to be true for
most folks. At least for me. When you are young
you just believe what you are told. As you get older
you begin to ask questions and look a little deeper
in order to find out what you really believe. After a
lot of research and personal searching, this is what I
believe to be true of God.

God is not a he a she or an it. God is the Presence of
Good and the Action of Love.

God is not a personification but a unification. The
unification of all that is good and all that is positive
and all that is love.

God is not mean or vengeful.

God doesn't care who wins the Super Bowl.

God doesn't think you are special, but thinks that
everyone and everything is perfect in every way just

the way it is, therefore there is no need for the word special. None is above another.

God loves you and accepts you just the way you are; there is no need to change in order to have approval.

God is not loving. To say that God is loving implies that God can be something other than love. God can't. God IS love.

God doesn't need to punish you and won't. You punish yourself enough, so God doesn't need to. We are not punished FOR our sins. We are punished BY our sins.

God does not judge. People judge. God accepts. You don't have to change for God to love you. However, you may have to change for people to love you.

God doesn't reward us based on our goodness. Goodness is the reward.

God has lots of things to say to you. But you usually have to get quiet to hear it. Your message from God is very private and very unique to you.

God believes in you.

God wants the best for you.

God wants you to be happy, successful, healthy and abundant in every way. It is not Godly to do without or to suffer. It is just the opposite. We are given incredible talents and abilities. Each and every one of us; no one is without these talents and abilities. They were given to us to use. Not to use them is a slap in the face to God.

God is more interested in you listening to God than in you talking to God. So many people are telling you to talk to God – and that is fine. I just believe that most of us talk way too much. It is more important to listen.

I speak at lots of banquets and luncheons and this is what is normally served to eat: something brown with white stuff on it or something white with brown stuff on it. That's all I know about it.

I ride in lots of cabs. I don't mind riding in cabs but I do have a couple of requests of cab drivers, not that many cab drivers are going to be reading this, but just in case you know a cab driver feel free to share these things with them.

1. If you drive a cab then help me with my luggage. Women should not take the job of a cab driver and then stand there with the trunk open waiting for me to pick up and load my own bag. If you take the job then do the whole job. (This is not a sexist comment, I don't care who drives my cab – I just want my bag loaded for me.)

2. Know where I am going. Especially if it is a major hotel. Don't rely on me to know the way.

3. If your air-conditioning or heater does not work then tell me *before* I get in and we have pulled away from the curb.

4. Have change. It isn't my job to get change from the bellman at the hotel or from the skycap at the airport.

5. Offer me a receipt. And give me an extra blank one.

6. Don't bore me with inane conversation. If I want to talk, then I will. If I don't then leave me alone.

7. Don't screw me. A clue is when the first question you ask me is, "Do you know the way?" Or "Have you ever been there before?" If I say no then the sucker gets taken for a ride. Don't do that. I am one of those guys who actually call and report it when I get screwed.

8. Don't smell. At all. Not good and not bad. I don't want to smell your sweat or your cologne or your cigarette smoke.

9. Clean your cab. I don't want to ride in a dirty cab. If it is dirty, it affects your tip.

10. Drive safely. I am not in that big of a hurry unless I tell you that I am. There is no reason for you to drive up the rear of the car in front of you. When I tell you not to, don't. If I tell you to slow down, do it. I am paying for the ride. If I don't like the ride, I won't pay for it.

11. Speak English. This is not a racist comment in any way. but if you are driving a cab in the United States, then you should be able to speak English. I don't care where you come from. I am glad that you are in this country and gainfully employed, that is more than many who were born here are doing so I applaud you. However, speak English. I promise you if I go to Abu Dhabi that I won't drive a cab until I can actually speak the local language.

Suggestion: Go to England. Look at the taxis. Take a couple of rides. That is how a taxicab system should work.

A magician was working on a cruise ship in the Caribbean. As the audience would be different each week, the magician allowed himself to do the same tricks over and over again. There was only one problem: the Captain's pet parrot saw the shows each week and eventually began to understand how the magician did every trick. Once he understood the tricks the parrot began yelling out in the middle of each show: "Look, it's not the same hat." "Look, he is hiding the flowers under table." "Hey, why are all the cards the Ace of Spades?" The magician was furious but couldn't do anything as it was the Captain's parrot. One day the ship had an accident and sank. The magician found himself floating on a piece of wood in the middle of the ocean with the parrot of course. They stared at each other with hate but did not utter a word to each other. This went on for a day and then another and then another. After a week, the parrot finally said, "Okay, I give up. Where's the boat?"

I like for things to make sense. They usually don't. Now that you can't take anything sharp on airplanes I am not able to take my pocket knife with me to cut open the boxes of books that we ship to my speaking engagements. So the other day I am on the airplane eating lunch. These days you don't get real knives to cut your food with, only those little plastic knives. But the plastic knife had a serrated edge and I knew I could use it to cut the tape on the boxes of books at the engagement when I got there so I stuck the plastic knife in my pocket. I had a connecting flight and as I was boarding I was once again searched whereupon they found the plastic knife. The poor things just went crazy because I had a knife and called their security supervisor over to talk to me. They explained that no knives were allowed on the plane. I explained that they had actually given me the knife on the plane. They said it didn't matter, that I couldn't take the knife on the plane. I told them that the flight I was about to get on was a meal flight and that they were going to give me another knife just like the one I already had on that plane so what difference did it make? They said no one was allowed to carry a knife aboard an airplane. That just doesn't make sense to me. Does it to you?

I'll try to be nicer, if you'll try to be smarter.

A few years ago I bought a Harley. I had never even been on a motorcycle in my life. But I had the attitude and the look and my partner, Vic, bought me a Harley t-shirt, so I had to get the bike. By the way, I agree with Jesse Ventura, a Harley is a bike, everything else is just a motorcycle. The interesting thing about riding a Harley is the camaraderie that goes on between Harley riders. First a Harley rider will always wave to another Harley rider. They don't know you, they just wave to prove the bond that exists between people who own Harleys. I think that's cool. And another thing: When you are at a place where guys who ride Harleys go, ummmmmm, let's see, that would be a biker bar I guess, you are always every other Harley rider's best friend. They don't care who you are or what you do, you are their friend. You can have a guy named Animal next to you covered from head to toe in tattoos and a doctor on the other side of you all acting like best friends. I think that is cool too. No judgment. No questions about who you are and how much money you make, just questions about your bike. The world should be more like a good biker bar.

So I'm doing a speech at some resort at a remote location in Tennessee. And I have to drive to get there. Now this is not my favorite thing to do. In fact, I wish all of my speeches were either in Las Vegas or at the Airport Hilton – someplace where I can just get off the plane, do the speech and move on. After a few hundred hotel rooms a year, no matter how special the hotel promises to be, it's just one more hotel room to me. But back to my story: I am driving along in the boonies of Tennessee and I keep passing these Yard Sale Ahead signs. I am not interested in actually going to the yard sale – I'm just noticing the signs. Finally, I see that the yard sale is right around the next bend in the road. As I round the bend I see three car doors propped up around a guy sitting in a lawn chair with a sign that says Yard Sale. That's the yard sale. Three car doors. Now that's funny. But not as funny as the guy who is also driving along past the yard sale looking at his car and saying to himself, "Hey, I could use me a car door." America. I love it.

How does the Gap get it and Neiman Marcus doesn't? How is it that you can teach a bunch of goofy minimum wage kids to greet customers and actually be helpful and you can't get a full-grown "sales professional" to acknowledge your presence, smile at you or say thank you?

The other day I am waiting to get on an airplane (pretty much how I spend most of time) and the plane is typically late. This guy goes ape and starts screaming and yelling at the poor gate agent (I don't usually speak so kindly of gate agents myself but this time they were truly innocent) about how poorly run the airline is, how stupid everyone there is, how ugly the airport is........you name it, this guy was screaming about. Finally he screamed out, "This is communism!" I had kept my mouth shut as long as I could. I approached him, tapped him on the shoulder and explained that a plane being late was a lot of things but communism was not one of them. I then politely told him that he was being loud and making an idiot out of himself. He said, "Who the hell do you think you are?" I told him I was the guy who had just told him that he was an idiot. He said, "Oh." And walked away. I then gave the rest of my bag of M&M's to the gate agent and apologized for all of the idiots in the world.

Please don't be an idiot – I am running out of apologies.

Can't people read? Moving sidewalks in airports clearly say "Stand Right – Walk Left." Is that a hard concept to grasp? I am walking along following this guy on the moving sidewalk and he is saying "excuse me, excuse me, excuse me" to a group of loudmouthed, overweight ex-jocks (you know the type) who were standing all over the thing and when they finally let this guy through one of them said, "Who does he think he is?" As I walked right between them a second later I said, "He's the guy who thinks you are smart enough to read the signs. Forgive him, he was wrong." Someday someone is going to beat the crap out of me.

You earn slack. No one is going to cut you slack so stop asking for people to cut you some slack. Why should they? Life does not issue Get Out Of Jail Free cards for being stupid. Stop expecting the world to rescue you. The Lone Ranger is not coming. Clean up your own mess. Fix your own problem. Admit that you are an idiot and commit to do better next time. Stop fixing the blame and start fixing the problem.

I am not an economist. I know very little about the stock market. But my opinion about the economy is that there is nothing wrong with the economy. It is just as it has always been. Sometimes it is good and sometimes it isn't. Things go up and things go down. The only problem with the economy is people's attitude toward it. I don't often, in fact, I think ever, agree with W but he was right when he said that we should get out there and spend some money. We should show confidence. If we think things are bad, then we will act as if things are bad and things will indeed get bad. So get out there and spend some money. Spend it with me and I'll go spend it somewhere else. I could use some new boots.

The President of a company I was hired to speak to called my office and insisted on talking to me. I rarely if ever do that. But somehow I agreed this time – I was standing right there anyway. He told me that he didn't want me to say anything about change. He said that he had promised his employees that change was over. I asked him if he really believed that. He said absolutely. I told him he was an idiot and that I couldn't speak to his group. He was a bit offended. Imagine that. But you know what? He really is an idiot. Now he is just an offended idiot. Change isn't a temporary condition. I wonder if he is still in business or whether he stopped being an idiot?

I am tired of people blaming movies, television, video games and music for the violence that goes on among children. It is a factor. But only a factor. What about lousy parenting? That is the real problem. If parents were involved in the lives of their children things would be different. Parents have left the parenting to the movies, TV, video games and music and then blame those things for the problem when it really is their own fault. You have to talk to your kids, play with them, take them places, let them know what you think is right and wrong, discipline them, tickle them, hug them, and even yell at them sometimes. Be a part of their lives. Know them. Know their friends. Don't blame others for the fact that your kids are a mess. If your kids are a mess, it is primarily because you are a lousy parent. There, I said it. Now deal with it.

I live in Paradise Valley, Arizona. Do you know why it's called Paradise Valley? Because it's paradise. Really it is. The best place on earth if you ask me, and though you didn't I am still telling you: it's the best place on earth. About half the time there is no weather – I mean it – it's so perfect that you don't even notice it. The other half it's hot. No, I mean HOT. HELL hot. The average temperature here for the whole month of July is 105 degrees. That is the average which means that many days it is much hotter. But they tell you it's a dry heat. So is my oven and I don't live there. But I do here. But it really is a dry heat. When you come from Oklahoma you understand that. In fact, if you come from anywhere in the South you will understand that. Because of the humidity. As you have heard before: It's not the heat, it's the humidity. That saying helped me figure out why I live in a place that is so hot. **It's not the heat, it's the stupidity.** And that saying is now available on a t-shirt at www.larrywinget.com – thank you!

There is no way to really end a book called ***thoughts and observations***. If you put The End it might mean that you have ended having thoughts and observations. Does that really happen? I hope not. I am always having thoughts and I am always making observations. In fact, since I stopped writing these things I have had lots of them. So I guess that the only appropriate way to end a book like this would be to just stop.

Larry Winget

Larry Winget is a philosopher of success who just happens to be hilarious. He teaches universal principles that will work for anyone, in any business, at any time, and does it by telling funny stories. He believes that most of us have complicated life and business way too much,  take it way too seriously and that we need to lighten up, take responsibility, be more flexible, stay positive and keep it in perspective. He believes that success and prosperity come from serving others. He teaches that business improves when the people in the business improve and that everything in life gets better when we get better and nothing gets better until we get better.

To have Larry speak to your organization or
to order any of his other personal and professional
development products contact:

Win Seminars!, Inc.
Tulsa, Oklahoma • Scottsdale, Arizona
800.749.4597

Or use the Internet:
www.larrywinget.com